KNOTS
&
SPLICES

KNOTS
&
SPLICES

Percy W. Blandford

BELL PUBLISHING COMPANY · NEW YORK

Contents

Introduction

There have always been knots. From the earliest days man has wanted to join ropes, vines, creepers and other flexible things. He has wanted to make things from these flexible materials. By trial and error over the years he has evolved a great many knots, hitches, splices, lashings and other fastenings. Today we can buy books showing how to make over 3,000 knots. The selection could be bewildering. There are whole chapters on knots for the same purpose. The beginner may be forgiven if he finds this too much and falls back on the granny knot for everything. There is a place for the large book which includes all the thousands of known knots, but in this book I hope to include only those which are essential, and those which are generally accepted as best for a purpose.

Ropes are made of a great variety of materials. Today the common ropes and cords in use are made of hemp, which is reasonably smooth to handle and quite strong. Cheaper rope is made of sisal. This is rough and whiskery. Much rough string is made of sisal. Cotton makes a smooth rope which is white when new, and easy on the hands, but it is not as strong as hemp. Several synthetic fibers are made into rope. These are manufactured plastics, and the best known are nylon and dacron. They

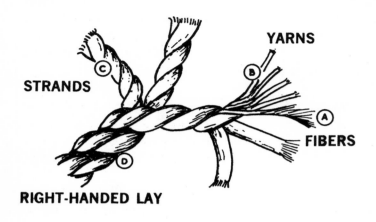

YARNS

STRANDS

FIBERS

RIGHT-HANDED LAY

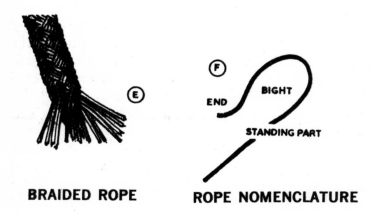

BRAIDED ROPE

ROPE NOMENCLATURE

END

BIGHT

STANDING PART

Figure 1

differ from the ropes made from natural fibers in being made from pieces of continuous lengths instead of short pieces. When new there is none of the whiskery feeling to the rope, although as they are used, some of the outside strands develop a hairy appearance. Nylon is more elastic than dacron. Cheap rope may be made of jute. Manila is a material very similar in appearance and strength to hemp. When it is necessary for a rope to float, it is made of coir, the same stuff as coconut matting. Coir is a weak material, so for equal strength a coir rope has to be much thicker than one made from other material.

If you examine a rope you can unravel it until you have the separate fibers (Fig. 1A). These are twisted together to form yarns (Fig. 1B). The yarns are twisted together to form strands (Fig. 1C). Most rope is made of three strands twisted together right-handed (Fig. 1D). As you look along the rope, the strands twist away from you to the right. The direction of twist is called the *lay* of the rope. If the strands are laid up right-handed, the yarns in each strand will be laid up left-handed. It is these two twists in opposition to each other that keep the rope in shape. Braided rope consists of the yarns plaited together around a heart made of other yarns, laid straight (Fig. 1E).

When a rope is doubled back into a loop, the end of the loop is known as a *bight,* whether the two parts cross each other or not (Fig. 1F). The part away from the end, which may be of any length, is known as the *standing part*. Strictly speaking, a *knot* is made in one piece of rope only; if you join two ropes together, you use a *bend;* and if you fasten the rope to a ring or post, you use a *hitch;* but there are so many exceptions to the rule that these terms cannot be relied on.

When a rope is cut, it very soon unlays itself, and you may have a foot or so of untidy wasted yarns. The end of every rope should be prevented from unlaying, and the simplest way of doing this is to put on a *whipping* (Fig. 1G). It is best to put on two temporary whippings before even cutting the rope. With expensive material, such as dacron, which soon unlays, this is most important. Cut ends of dacron and nylon can be prevented from unlaying by heating with a flame so that the material melts and runs together. However, a whipping is still desirable, and is essential with the other materials.

As with knots, there are a great many whippings. Not more than three will serve most people. For normal ropes, stout thread is thick enough for whippings. The type sold as *sail twine* is suitable, although colored carpet thread is attractive. The thread is helped to stay put and is waterproofed if it is drawn through a piece of beeswax or a candle before use.

To make a *common whipping,* put a short length of the line along the rope towards the end and put some tight turns over it (Fig. 1G). Continue until the whipping is almost as long as the thickness of the rope, then double back the end (Fig. 1H). Put on another three turns and pass the working end through the little loop (Fig. 1I). Pull projecting end so as to draw both parts under the turns, then cut off the surplus line (Fig. 1J).

With practice the common whipping is quickly made, but it is not as secure as the other two, and is best regarded as only temporary. An alternative is the *West Country whipping.* The middle of the line is put behind the rope, then the two ends are knotted tightly in front (Fig. 1K). Make another knot behind and continue knotting in front and behind along the rope (Fig. 1L). When the whipping is about as long as the thickness of the rope, make the last knot into a reef knot (Fig. 1M).

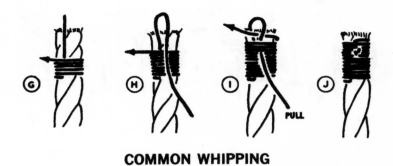

COMMON WHIPPING

WEST COUNTRY WHIPPING

Figure 1 *(cont.)*

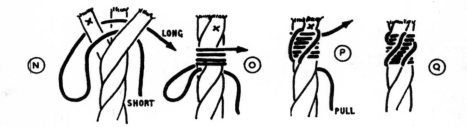

SAILOR'S WHIPPING

Figure 1 *(cont.)*

The strongest whipping, *sailor's whipping,* has the line passing through the rope. There is a method of doing this with a needle, but the sailor's whipping gets the same result without any tools. Open the strands for a short distance and lay in a loop of whipping line so that it encircles one strand and the two ends come out together through the opposite space. One end can be quite short (Fig. 1N). Lay up the strands carefully, and hold the loop and the short end along the rope, out of the way, while you put on the whipping turns with the long end (Fig. 1O). Notice which end strand already has the loop around it below the whipping, then lift the loop over its top and pull the short end (Fig. 1P). This will put *snaking* turns up the outside of the whipping. Let the short end follow up the outside of the space it is projecting from, to make a third snaking turn, and tie it to the long end in the middle of the end of the rope (Fig. 1Q) and cut off.

1
Basic Knots

Whatever your reason for learning knots, there are several that are common to all ropework, and it is as well to master their construction thoroughly. Once the knot is known, it should be practiced in various circumstances. You may have to use the knot in the dark. It might be needed under water. Perhaps you will have to tie it with your mouth and one hand, while holding on with the other. Practice these things. It is entertaining, as well as instructive, to practice making knots with a companion, using *only one hand each!*

The one knot which everyone knows about, but does not always tie, is the *reef,* or *square knot.* Does the bow of your shoe lace or apron string run up and down or across? If up and down, it is a *granny* and not the reef you probably imagined. If you make a knot between two ends by twisting them together twice in the same direction, this is a granny (Fig. 2A), with the ends across the direction of pull. It may hold. It may not. You cannot rely on a granny. Instead, twist the second part in the opposite direction to the first and you have a reef knot (Fig. 2B). It may be useful to remember "right-over-left, left-over-right." A reef knot is a good general-purpose joining knot, but it is only satisfactory when bearing against something. If one or both ends are turned back into bights when making the second part, the result is a *slip reef* (Fig. 2C) or *bow,* which is easily undone.

GRANNY KNOT

REEF (SQUARE) KNOT

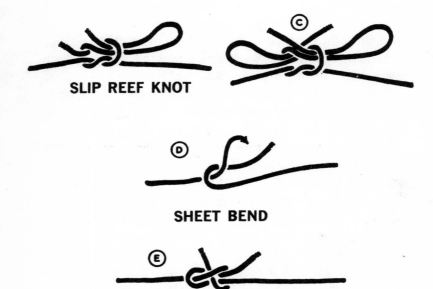

SLIP REEF KNOT

SHEET BEND

Figure 2

If two ropes have to be joined merely to make them longer and the knot will not bear against anything, it is better to use a sheet bend. One end is turned back into a bight, then the other taken up through it (Fig. 2D), around the back and across the front of the bight, under itself (Fig. 2E). It is debatable which is the best way to go round, but there is little to choose in strength. If the ropes are of two different thicknesses, the thicker should be the one made into a bight. If there is a very great difference in thickness, go round twice to make a double sheet bend (Fig. 2F).

The classic knot for making a loop is the *bowline*. This will not slip, yet is easily undone after being under load. The basic method of making a bowline is to take the amount needed and form a little loop in the standing part. Take the working end through this, going in on the same side as the standing part is (Fig. 2G). Go around the standing part and back down through the little loop (Fig. 2H). Pull tight by holding the sides of the loop and the short end together, while pulling in the opposite direction with the standing part. Incorrect tightening will distort the knot.

A quicker method of making the bowline around your own waist or any other object, such as a post, is to put the end over the standing part (Fig. 2I) and twist it over and away from the main loop (Fig. 2J), pulling it hard so that the end pulls straight and a small loop is made in the standing part, leaving the knot almost finished (Fig. 2K).

A knot made in a rope to prevent it pulling through your hand or a hole, is called a *stopper knot*. The simplest has many names, but may be best known as an *overhand knot* (Fig. 2L). If this is not sufficiently bulky, there can be an extra turn, forming a *figure eight* (Fig.

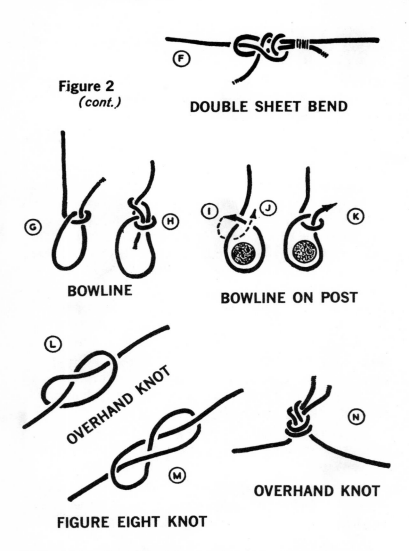

Figure 2
(cont.)

(F) **DOUBLE SHEET BEND**

(G) (H) **BOWLINE**

(I) (J) (K) **BOWLINE ON POST**

(L) OVERHAND KNOT

(M) **FIGURE EIGHT KNOT**

(N) **OVERHAND KNOT**

2M). Either knot may be used to join lines, but this is not recommended. The overhand knot may be satisfactory for cotton (Fig. 2N), but it is not advised for joining larger stuff, as it puts such a sharp twist into the line where it enters the knot that the material is weakened.

A very useful variation of the figure eight knot is the *packer's knot,* which the man behind the counter uses to tie up your parcel. It is a slip knot which can be pulled tight and locked. A figure eight knot is made with the end around the standing part. Take care that this finishes with the end standing up (Fig. 3A), and not the other way. The line is tightened by pulling on the standing part, then a little loop, called a *half hitch,* is made with the standing part over the end projecting from the figure eight knot (Fig. 3B).

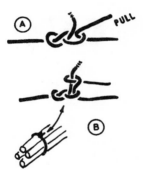

PACKER'S KNOT

Figure 3

Many knots for fastening ropes to spars or rings depend on jamming half hitches together in various ways. The basic fastening of this type is a *clove hitch.* The end is taken around the spar and over the standing part (Fig. 3C). It continues around the same way, and next time it comes to the front, it is passed under itself (Fig. 3D). A common fault is to change direction after the first time round (Fig. 3E). The result is called a *lark's head,* and is seen on luggage label strings. It has other uses, but

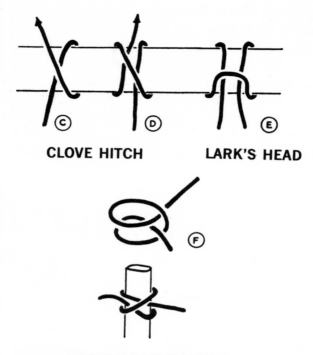

CLOVE HITCH   **LARK'S HEAD**

DOUBLE CLOVE HITCH

Figure 3 *(cont.)*

it is not an alternative to the clove hitch. If the end of a post is accessible, the clove hitch can be slipped over the end ready-made. Two similar loops are made (Fig. 3F) and put over each other so that the ends project from inside; then they are dropped over the post. This is called a *double clove hitch*.

The clove hitch is often used as an end fastening, but it is only really safe when there is a load on both ends. For fastening the end of a rope to a spar or ring it is better to use a *round turn* and two half hitches. Completely encircle the spar or ring with the working end

(Fig. 3G). This is the round turn. Keep a strain on the standing part, then use the end to put a clove hitch around it (Fig. 3H).

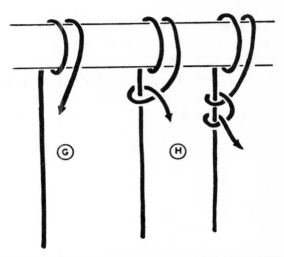

ROUND TURN AND TWO HALF HITCHES

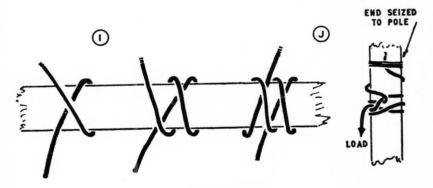

ROLLING HITCH

Figure 3 *(cont.)*

Neither of these knots is very satisfactory if the pull on the standing part is along the spar, because the turns tend to slip. It is better to make a *rolling hitch,* which is really a clove hitch with an extra turn. After taking the working end around and over the standing part, go round again (Fig. 3I), also over the standing part. Continue to make the other half hitch as in a clove hitch (Fig. 3J). The load should come on the part that is covered by two turns. For the greatest strength, the free end may be taken around the spar and seized to it with a few turns of light line.

2
Outdoor Knotting

Anyone interested in camping, exploring and other outdoor activity will find plenty of use for knots. Guy lines for tents may be fashioned. Pioneering projects may be tackled. Knotting may have to be done in anything from string to hawsers.

If a rope has to be attached to a rough log, the best knot is a simple slip knot, called a *timber hitch*. The end is taken back around the standing part and twisted around itself at least three times (Fig. 4A). If you wish to drag the log, another half hitch will keep the pull end on (Fig. 4B).

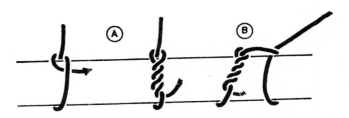

TIMBER HITCH AND A HALF HITCH

Figure 4

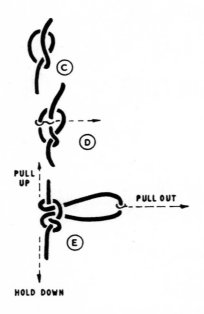

MAN-HARNESS KNOT   **Figure 4**
                                   (*cont.*)

For dragging, you can get your shoulder into a bowline at the end of the rope, but if someone is needed to
help you, you have to make a loop in the rope without
using its ends. This can be a *man-harness knot*. Take
up enough for the loop (Fig. 4C), and start to make
an overhand knot in it (Fig. 4D). Instead of completing
the overhand knot, grasp the opposite side of the loop
through the part-knot and pull it through (Fig. 4E). To
keep the knot in shape while doing this, hold one part of
the rope under your foot while pulling upwards on the
other part, and outwards at right angles on the loop.

The *sheepshank* is usually used for shortening a rope.
It is, but another important use is for strengthening a

SHEEPSHANK

Figure 4
(cont.)

Ⓕ   Ⓖ

LOAD

Ⓗ

PULL

LEVERAGE SHEEPSHANK

Ⓘ

OVERHAND

Ⓙ

FIGURE EIGHT

Ⓚ

RUNNER

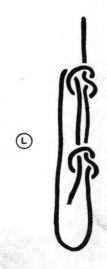

Ⓛ

GUY LINE HITCH

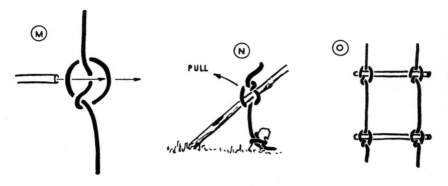

MARLINSPIKE OR LEVER HITCH

Figure 4 *(cont.)*

weak part. If the rope is frayed, gather it up into a long S-shape with the weak part in the center (Fig. 4F). At both ends put half hitches over the loops (Fig. 4G). A variation on the sheepshank can be used to obtain leverage, and may often be seen on the ropes over loads on trucks. A sheepshank is formed, with a half hitch only on the end about to take the strain. The end of the rope is taken around something solid and back through the long loop and pulled (Fig. 4H). This gives a theoretical advantage of two to one, but friction reduces this.

Guy lines may be fixed with overhead knots through eyelets (Fig. 4I). In lightweight tents, figure eight knots may be used (Fig. 4J). If runners slip too easily, they may be tightened by reversing the direction of the rope through them (Fig. 4K). If a runner is missing, a guy line hitch can be made with the end taken back through two overhand knots (Fig. 4L).

A useful simple knot is the *marlin spike* or *lever hitch*. To increase the grip when pulling a rope, a piece of wood may be pushed across a partly-formed overhand knot (Fig. 4M). The same idea may be used to lever out tent pegs (Fig. 4N). A series of these hitches may be used to make a rope ladder (Fig. 4O).

A double loop is needed sometimes for accommodating a special load or for lowering a man by supporting him under his knees and armpits. If one rope is to take the load and a part has to hang below to guide it, the knot to choose is the *fireman's chair knot*. Take two loops as if to make a clove hitch (Fig. 5A). Pull the overlapping parts through the opposite loops, adjusting them to the needed sizes. (Fig. 5B). Secure with half hitches (Fig. 5C), run up close to the center.

If both parts of the rope are to take the load, it is better to use a *bowline-on-a-bight*. Take a long bight of

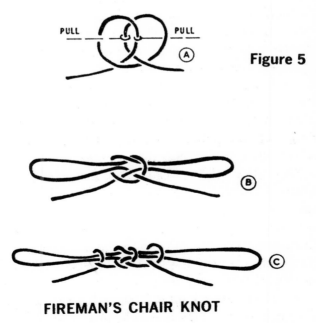

Figure 5

FIREMAN'S CHAIR KNOT

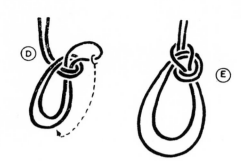

Figure 5
(cont.)

BOWLINE-ON-A-BIGHT

rope and make a small loop in it, as for an ordinary bowline. Put the end of the bight through this (Fig. 5D). Without distorting the rest of the knot, bend the end of the bight back and pass it around the rest of the knot, so as to finish around the standing parts (Fig. 5E).

When camping, it is often necessary to lash poles and spars together. These may be little structures of string and twigs for a plate rack, or parts of a substantial bridge. The method is the same. Nearly all of this type of ropework can be done with three lashings, which are easy to apply.

Where two spars cross and have to be joined, even if not at right angles, and normal loads might try to make them slide over each other, the *square lashing* is used. The end of the line is fastened around the spar nearest upright with a clove hitch and the loose end twisted around the standing part (Fig. 5F). Take the line around the spars squarely three or four times (Fig. 5G), putting on as much strain as you can at all stages—it is no use depending on pulling tight only at the end.

Further tightening is done with *frapping* turns, put on between the spars, pulled taut (Fig. 5H), and finished after three or four turns wtih a clove hitch on the other spar (Fig. 5I).

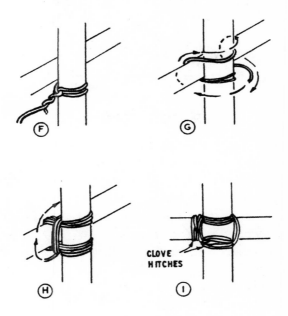

CLOVE
HITCHES

SQUARE LASHING

Figure 5 (*cont.*)

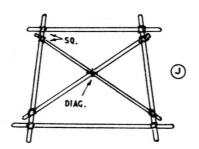

FRAME LASHINGS

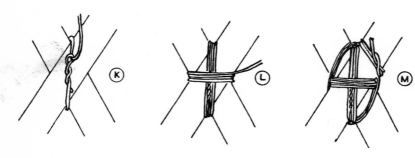

DIAGONAL LASHING

Figure 5 (*cont.*)

A four-sided structure may push out of shape. A triangle cannot be pushed out of shape, so it is usual in pioneering to make everything into triangles. This is done in a basic framework by adding two diagonals (Fig. 5J)—*diagonal lashing*. The ends of the diagonals are held by square lashings, but where they cross and any distorting strain might tend to pull them apart, they are held by a diagonal lashing. A timber hitch is put on diagonally (Fig. 5K), followed by three or four turns in one direction and three or four the other way (Fig. 5L). Frapping turns tighten the lashing, and the line is finished with a clove hitch on one of the spars (Fig. 5M).

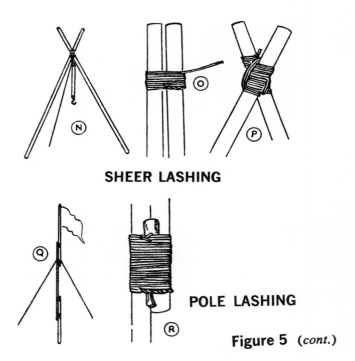

SHEER LASHING

POLE LASHING

Figure 5 (*cont.*)

When two spars are made into sheer legs to lift a weight or support a bridge (Fig. 5N), a *sheer lashing* is used. Start with a clove hitch and put on turns around the spars held parallel (Fig. 5O). Pull them slightly apart and put on three or four frapping turns (Fig. 5P) before finishing with another clove hitch.

If poles have to be lashed to increase their length, as when improvising a flagstaff (Fig. 5Q), a variation of the sheer lashing is used. This is called *pole lashing*. The clove hitch goes around both spars at the start, then after the turns are put on tightly there is another clove hitch at the other end (Fig. 5R). As it is difficult to put frapping turns between parallel spars, the lashing may be tightened by driving in wooden wedges.

3
Boating Knots

Most of the thousands of knots were devised by seamen. The heyday of their use was in the days of square-rigged sailing ships, when much fancy knotting was practiced besides the pure utility knots which were essential to the management of the ship. Those days are gone, but anyone who goes afloat for business or pleasure today needs to know a few knots thoroughly. A boy or girl in his first dinghy or canoe should take a pride in proper whippings and splices and the right knot correctly made at the right time. There was a saying that a ship is known by her ropes, and that still applies today.

The basic knots already described are the essential ones for small boating. Many of the other knots described for other purposes also have their application afloat. For instance, the timber hitch (Fig. 4A and B) can be used to make an anchor from a heavy stone. With the half hitch close up to the timber hitch, this is known at sea as a *killick hitch* (Fig. 6A)—"killick" being a name for an anchor.

When a rope is used as an anchor cable, it must be attached to the anchor ring securely because you cannot inspect it in use. The *fisherman's bend,* or *anchor bend,* is used for this job (Fig. 6B). It is a round turn and two half-hitches (Fig. 3G and H), with the first part of the

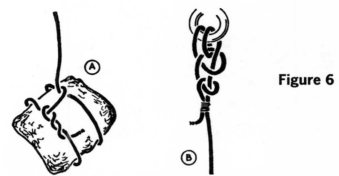

Figure 6

TIMBER HITCH AND HALF HITCH-KILLICK HITCH

FISHERMAN'S BEND OR ANCHOR BEND

clove hitch taking up the middle of the round turn. When this knot has pulled tight and is wet, it is very difficult to undo.

A rope anchor cable is usually fixed inboard with a shackle, and there is a post or bollard to fasten to when the anchor is down. The knot used here must be one which is easily let go in an emergency. A bight of rope can be taken around (Fig. 6C), under both parts of the rope under strain (Fig. 6D), and over the top of the post (Fig. 6E). Ashore, this same knot is better than a clove hitch for making a fence by slinging a rope between posts.

MAKING FAST TO A BITT OR POST

Figure 6 (*cont.*)

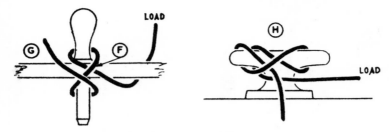

BELAYING TO A PIN OR CLEAT

Figure 6 (*cont.*)

"Belaying" means making a line fast to a cleat or be-laying pin. Even on the smallest sailing boat there will be one halyard to be fastened in this way. It is best to make a turn to take the first strain (Fig. 6F) before putting on one or two turns figure eight fashion (Fig. 6G). In many cases it is safest to merely rely on these turns to hold, so that they can be let go quickly if necessary. In some cases a loop of the end part can be jammed temporarily under the standing part. Where the fastening has to be more securely finished, a half hitch can be put over one end of the belaying pin or cleat (Fig. 6H).

The *carrick bend* (Fig. 6I) is a strong joining knot suitable for all thicknesses of line, although it is often only considered for really large ropes. It does not jam even when wet. A bight of one rope is crossed and the other worked around it (Fig. 6J), using a regular over-and-under action (Fig. 6K). At no point does the rope pass through a loop and the ends finish on opposite sides. With large hawsers it is usual to seize the ends down to the standing parts with a few turns of light line. This keeps the knot in a round flexible form which will pass through a hole or around a bollard. With lighter lines the knot can be allowed to distort as it tightens without weakening the joint.

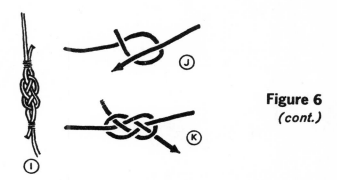

Figure 6
(cont.)

CARRICK BEND

It is sometimes helpful if the boat's painter can be made fast in a way that allows quick release, as when preparing to get under way with an outboard motor while a fast current is flowing. A good slippery hitch for this occasion is a *highwayman's,* or *painter hitch,* which was supposed to have been used to tie a horse ready for a quick getaway. A bight of the painter is passed around the post or through the ring (Fig. 6L). A second bight in the part under load is put through this first bight, which is pulled tight (Fig. 6M). Next, a bight in the free part of the rope is put through this second bight, which is pulled tight on to it (Fig. 6N). This completes the hitch, which cannot be undone by the pulling of the boat, although a jerk on the free end will release it.

When getting a tow in a boat, it is important that the tow-rope should be easily let go if necessary. Rather than use a firm knot, it is better to lead the rope to a thwart, where a couple of turns are taken and bight of the rope then tucked under (Fig. 7A)—*towing hitch.* A jerk on the end will release the tow.

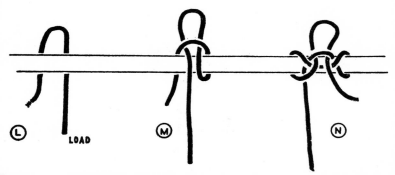

Figure 6 **HIGHWAYMAN'S HITCH (PAINTER HITCH)**
(cont.) To fasten a rope to a hook, a *catspaw* is useful. The end of a bight is thrown back over the two parts of the rope (Fig. 7B). Wtih a hand on each end part they are twisted in opposite directions, usually three times, then the loops slipped over the hook (Fig. 7C). This knot keeps its shape best when there is a load on both ends, but it is secure when the load comes on only one end.

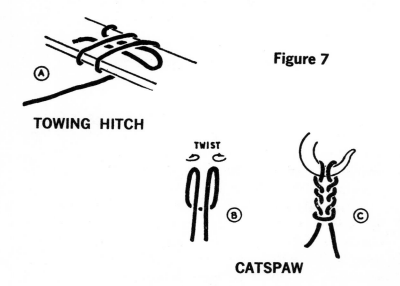

Figure 7

TOWING HITCH

CATSPAW

(D)

Figure 7
(*cont.*)

MOUSING

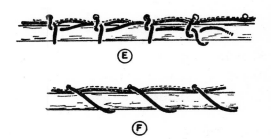

(E)

(F)

MARLING

If a hook with a rope on is liable to jerking and there is a risk of the rope coming off, it is *moused* with light line, clove hitched on and taken several times across the opening. Turns are made around these strands and the mousing finished with another clove hitch (Fig. 7D).

When sails are laced to spars with a continuous line, the process is called *marling*. It is also useful for pulling bundles together and similar purposes. The important thing is to see that each action tucks under, locking at each crossing (Fig. 7E) and not merely loosely looped each time (Fig. 7F).

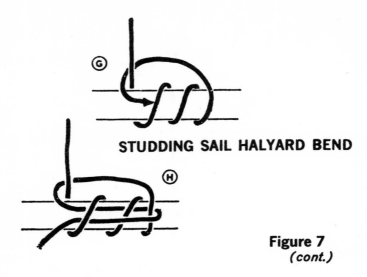

STUDDING SAIL HALYARD BEND

Figure 7
(cont.)

In a simple sailing rig the yard or gaff has to be hauled up close to the mast sheave by a halyard knotted around it. If the knot has to be completed by working around the standing part, as in a round turn and two half hitches, the spar cannot be pulled close to the mast. For this purpose there is the *studding sail halliard bend*. It is started like a fisherman's bend, with a second round turn and the end passed under the center (Fig. 7G) before tucking again under the first turn (Fig. 7H).

It is sometimes necessary to sling a short plank as a bos'n's chair for work up a mast, or a longer plank for work over the side of the boat. For both purposes there is the *scaffold hitch*. The rope is wrapped around the end of the plank so that there are three parts on top (Fig. 7I). Part 1 is lifted over part 2 (Fig. 7J), then part 2 is eased up and over the end of the plank (Fig. 7K). The two parts are then brought up to tighten the hitch and joined together in a bowline (Fig. 7L). Of course, the same is done at the other end of the plank.

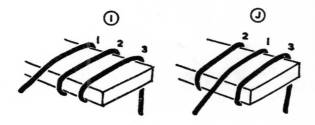

SCAFFOLD HITCH

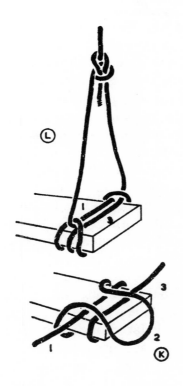

Figure 7 *(cont.)*

4

Angler's Knots

The fisherman, whether his interest is in fresh-water sport with rod and line or in more ambitious deep-sea fishing, is faced with knotting problems different from those of others who need knots. Most of the material he has to knot is very thin, and much of it is very smooth and slippery. With the coming of nylon and other synthetic lines, this problem of slipperiness is even more acute. Consequently, the knots needed by the angler are rather specialized, although there are occasions when he can use the basic knots.

The simplest way of making a loop on the end of a cast is to double it back and tie an overhand knot (Fig. 8A). With slippery material it is better to do the same thing with the extra turn of a figure eight knot (Fig. 8B). It may even be advisable to put in another turn to make a *blood bight knot* (Fig. 8C).

A loop made by one of these knots does not finish exactly in line with the standing part. A knot which keeps the loop in line is made with two overhand knots. Make one overhand knot far enough back from the end to allow for the loop, and pass the end down through it (Fig. 8D). With the end, make another overhand knot around the standing part (Fig. 8E). Make both knots in such a way that the twisted parts finish parallel with the

OVERHAND

FIGURE EIGHT

BLOOD BIGHT KNOT

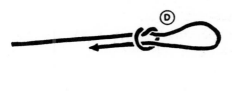

LOOP WITH DOUBLE OVERHAND KNOTS

Figure 8

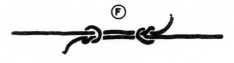

FISHERMAN'S KNOT

FISHERMAN'S KNOT AND HALF HITCHES

BARREL KNOT

Figure 8
(cont.)

straight part, instead of across, as will happen if twisted the other way. If this is done, the two overhand knots fit into each other when the loop is drawn tight.

A similar knot is used for joining line, and this is best known as the *fisherman's knot* (Fig. 8F). One end is passed through an overhand knot in the end of the other line, then knotted around it. After pulling tight, it is advisable to put on a half hitch with each end before cutting off (Fig. 8G).

The simple fisherman's knot is not as popular as the *barrel and blood knots,* which have many variations but which have the advantage of more turns to resist slipping. A barrel knot is based on the fisherman's knot, but when each overhand knot is made, it is given an extra turn (Fig. 8H).

To make a blood knot, hold the overlapping lines at what will be the center of the knot, then wrap one end three times around the other part and back through the center (Fig. 8I). While still holding the center, do the same with the other end. This will make a symmetrical knot, with the two ends projecting from opposite sides of the center (Fig. 8J). Make sure the twists on both sides are made in the same direction. Draw up carefully and tightly before cutting off.

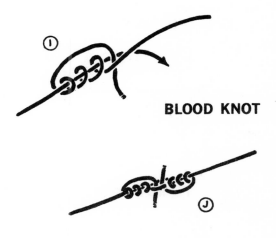

BLOOD KNOT

Figure 8 *(cont.)*

A *half blood knot* may be used to attach a swivel. The line is taken through the swivel and given three or four turns around the standing part (Fig. 8K) before taking it back through the part nearest the swivel (Fig. 8L). Draw up carefully, so as to keep the shape.

HALF BLOOD KNOT

Figure 8 *(cont.)*

A sheet bend does not have enough turns to resist slipping in fishing line. It can be improved, *modified sheet bend,* if, after forming in the usual way (Fig. 9A), the end is taken back around itself before tightening (Fig. 9B).

If a fly length or other *branch line* has to be attached, a simple way is to use a knotted end through the center

MODIFIED SHEET BEND

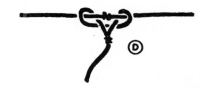

ATTACHING BRANCH LINES

Figure 9

of any of the joining knots (Fig. 9C). Another way, which helps to make the branch lines stand well out, is to have an overhand knot in the main line to locate the branch, which is fixed around it with what is really a lark's head knot (Fig. 9D).

The basic knot for attaching a line to a hook or a fly is a simple half hitch (Fig. 9E), but this will not hold a modern slippery line. Developments are based on the overhand (Fig. 9F) and figure eight knots (Fig. 9G). The important thing is to build up a lump which cannot pull through the eye, and which has sufficient friction to resist slipping undone.

HALF HITCH   OVERHAND

FIGURE EIGHT

Figure 9 *(cont.)*

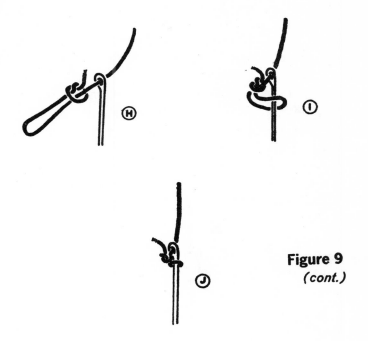

Figure 9
(cont.)

BASIC TURLE KNOT

Another series of knots for attaching hooks or flies is known as *turle knots*. In the *basic turle knot*, the line is passed through the eye, then a running loop is made in the end (Fig. 9H). The knot is pulled almost tight, then the hook passed through the loop (Fig. 9I), and the line pulled (Fig. 9J), leaving one turn around the back of the hook and the bulk of the knot against the eye.

For modern materials it is better to put in an extra turn to make a *two-turn turle knot*. Twist the end around twice (Fig. 9K). Draw it up to leave the loop (Fig. 9L). Pass the hook through the loop and draw tight (Fig. 9M).

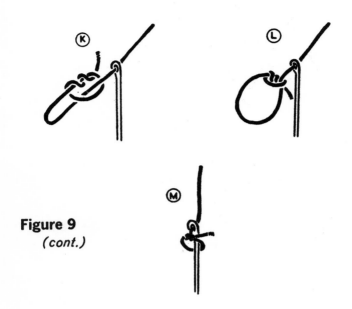

Figure 9
(cont.)

TWO-TURN TURLE KNOT

Netmaking is not difficult. If the joint between meshes in an ordinary net is examined, it will be seen to be an ordinary sheet bend. Netmaking consists of tying sheet bends. Few tools are needed. A small amount of netting can be done without tools, but two simple tools give speed and accuracy. One is a piece of wood, of no particular length, but of a width to suit the desired length of the side of a mesh (Fig. 10A). The other is a shuttle or needle on which the line may be wound and worked. Simplest is a wood, even card, H-shaped piece (Fig. 10B). This is better if the ends curve inwards (Fig. (10C). A different type has a central spike around which the line is taken from opposite sides (Fig. 10D).

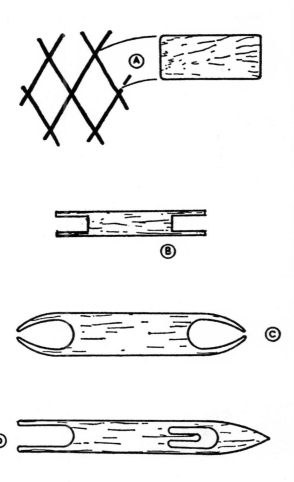

NETMAKING TOOLS

Figure 10

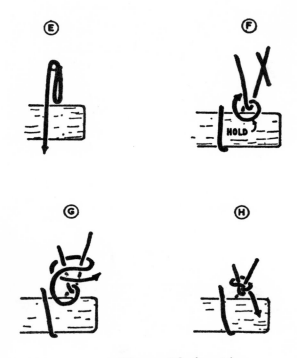

Figure 10 *(cont.)*

Wind a shuttleful of line, then make a bowline in its end of the same length as the meshes are to be. Hook this over a nail. Hold the gauge against the bottom of the bowline, and bring the line down in front of it (Fig. 10E). Pass the shuttle up through the bottom of the bowline, and hold the line against the gauge with the left thumb (Fig. 10F). Pass the shuttle behind the loop and across the front, under the part being held by the thumb (Fig. 10G). Pull tight, but be careful that the knot keeps its shape (Fig. 10H) and the part just worked does not slip down below the loop when tightening.

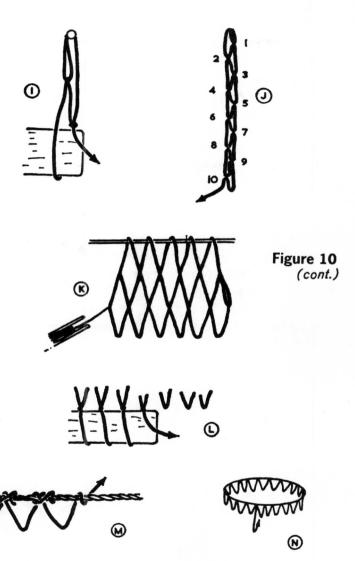

Figure 10
(cont.)

NET-MAKING

Move the gauge down to the bottom of the mesh just formed and repeat the actions (Fig. 10I). Continue in this way until a chain of sufficient meshes for the head of the net has been made (Fig. 10J). This actually forms the first two rows. Thread a rod through the top row and support it so that the working end is on the left (Fig. 10K). Hold the mesh gauge against the bottoms of the meshes and start making new meshes around it. They need not be removed each time, but can slide across the gauge (Fig. 10L). At the end of the row, turn the work over so as to bring the working end to the left again.

Nets may be started with a head rope or rod to which they are clove-hitched (Fig. 10M). For a round net on a metal ring, after each complete circuit of meshes the line will have to drop down to start the next mesh (Fig. 10N). The simplest way to close the bottom of such a net is by a draw string.

If a net has to be repaired, examine it to see which way up the knots are. Cut out the damaged meshes fairly close to the knots, then work in new meshes with similar line. It may be necessary to cut out a few sound meshes so as to be able to work a regular pattern with the new line and avoid too many joins.

5
Climber's Knots

The climber and mountaineer needs knots on which he can depend and which are as near foolproof as possible. As with the angler, some of the accepted climber's knots have had to be modified to suit the smoother ropes produced from synthetic materials. It is even more important with these new materials to pull each knot tight and into the correct shape before it takes a strain.

Most climbers wrap a rope several times around their waist. This may be joined with an ordinary reef knot, but for extra security the ends should be tucked through the rope (Fig. 11A).

With ordinary rope many of the knots already described may be used. The bowline around the waist or attached to the karibiner is satisfactory. In synthetic rope there is a *Tarbuck knot,* named after its inventor. Although it is a slip knot, the friction of the many turns prevents its slipping except under very great load. It is claimed that then the slight movement acts as a shock absorber. There is a family likeness to some of the angler's knots. It should be practiced to ensure correct formation each time. The end is taken several times around the standing part towards the loop (Fig. 11B), then back over the turns to make a figure eight lock (Fig. 11C). The formation of this last action is most important. If

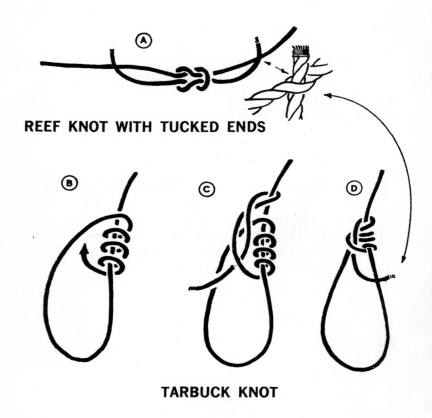

REEF KNOT WITH TUCKED ENDS

TARBUCK KNOT

Figure 11

used around the waist, the end should be tucked through the rope to limit any shock-absorbing slip (Fig. 11D).

Loops for a middle man are not so popular today; it is more usual for the second man to be joined to the first and third by separate ropes. If a middle man is to join into a continuous rope, it is best to use a short continuous loop which is clipped to his karibiner. This is

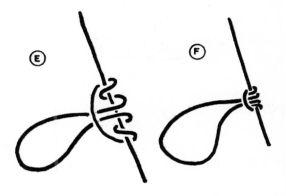

PRUSIK KNOT

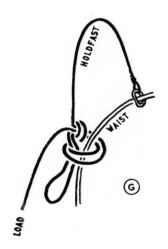

FIGURE EIGHT IN A BIGHT

Figure 11 *(cont.)*

joined in with a *prusik knot.* The loop is taken twice round the main rope, then the projecting part tucked under (Fig. 11E). Pull it tight so that the turns rest evenly around the main rope (Fig. 11F). If the loop has to be made by joining the ends of a short piece, it is best to splice them, although a fisherman's knot could be used, providing it is kept away from the turns bearing on the main rope.

If a knot is needed to anchor back the rope to the waist band, a figure eight knot may be made in a bight of it (Fig. 11G).

6

Splicing

When something more permanent than a simple knot is needed in a rope, a splice is called for. The one most frequently used is the *eye splice,* but the *back splice* is easiest to learn and the *short splice* is essential for permanently joining two ropes. There are many other splices, but these three will take care of most people's needs. The ability to splice allows you to make workmanlike jobs of such things as lanyards, guy lines and rigging. A permanent piece of ropework is much better with splices than with knots. While a bowline is a perfectly good knot, an eye splice is neater and smarter when a permanent loop is needed in the rope.

A back splice is a means of turning the strands of a rope back on themselves to prevent the end of the rope fraying. It is an alternative to a whipping, but, as it increases the thickness of the rope at the end, it is not as suitable for situations where the rope will have to pass through a hole or around a sheave in a pulley block.

A back splice in three-stranded rope is started by unlaying the strands for a short distance. Form them into a crown knot (Fig. 12A). Take each over its neighbor on the right and under the next, if it is right-handed rope. Pull up tight evenly, so that the ends form a star across the end of the rope.

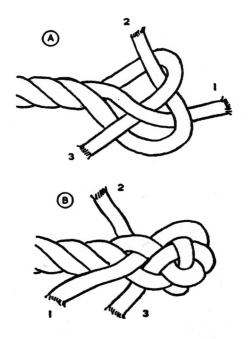

BACK SPLICE

Figure 12

Each end strand will be found to be pointing across a strand in the main body of the rope. Lift the next main strand sufficiently to tuck an end strand under it. Do this at all three positions (Fig. 12B), so that each end strand goes over and under one main strand. Repeat this, taking each end in turn over the strand beside it and under the next one. Do it once more, so that each end is tucked three times. Go around the rope at about the same angle as the lay of the rope, although in the opposite direction. A common fault is to tuck almost straight down the rope. Three tucks are usually sufficient, but for neatness about

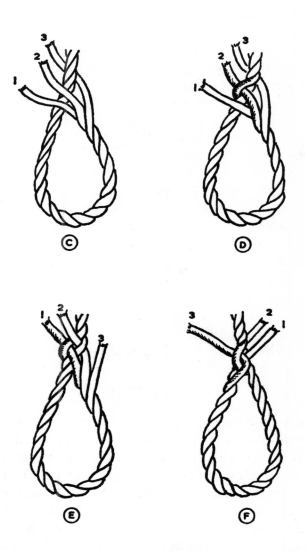

EYE SPLICE

Figure 12 *(cont.)*

half the fibers may be scraped out of each strand with a sharp knife, then one more tuck made to give a tapered finish.

The eye splice may be made as a loop of any size, or it can be made tight around a metal thimble or a wooden toggle. A thimble protects the rope from chafe and is often used for shackling ropes to fittings on boats and elsewhere. A toggle makes a quick joint into another eye splice, and is often fitted to the top of a flag. Practice eye splices should be made as free loops, as a little experience is needed to fit them correctly around solid things.

Unlay the strands for a short distance and double the rope back to form a loop, with the unlaid ends pointing across the lay of the rope. Regard this as the front (Fig. 12C). Take one of the ends and tuck it under any of the main strands. Arrange the next one to it on the loop side across the rope and push the third one out of the way behind (Fig. 12D). Take the second one under the next strand to the first one, going in where the first one comes out (Fig. 12E).

Turn the splice over. There is one end strand left, and one main strand without an end strand under it. The end does not have to go in the way it is pointing, but must go under the strand against the lay (Fig. 12F), so that it is pointing the same way around the rope as the other ends. See that all three ends come out level with each other and are equally tensioned. Tuck each end again, over one and under one, in the same way as in the back splice. Even up the tension, then tuck once more. Taper a further tuck if you wish. Any splice can be rolled smooth between two boards, preferably before trimming off the ends of the strands. Rolling is sometimes done on the floor under the shoe, but this is liable to press grit into the fibers.

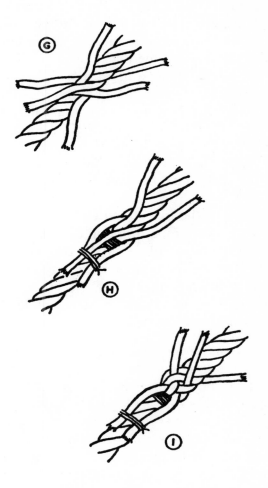

SHORT SPLICE

Figure 12 *(cont.)*

A short splice is used for joining ropes, but as it increases the thickness it has the same disadvantage as the back splice if the rope has to pass through a restricted space. As its name implies, there is also a long splice. This does not increase the thickness of the rope appreciably, but it is rarely used in practice.

To make a short splice, unlay both ropes for a short distance and bring them together so that each end comes in a space of the other rope (Fig. 12G). For a first short splice it is a help to put a whipping on one rope and temporarily seize the opposing strands over it. In this way half of the splice may be done first without confusion (Fig. 12H).

Take each of the free strand ends over and under a strand of the other rope, working against the lay (Fig. 12I), as in the other splices. Make two whole tucks in this way. Remove the temporary seizing and whipping and make two whole tucks with the other three ends. This total of four tucks should be sufficient, but for neatness there may be taper tucks at each end.

7
Special Knots

Of the large number of knots, those listed under other headings are considered the most appropriate for their purposes. Those listed in this chapter have their own special uses and are worth learning.

If one rope has to pull another rope through a confined space, such as a hole, any of the usual joining knots with ends at opposite sides may catch on the way through. For this purpose there is a *binder turn* (Fig. 13A), which can be seen to be a sheet bend with the end tucked the other way.

If a very thin line has to tow a very thick line, as when a heaving line is used to pull a hawser, the thick rope is bent into a bight and the thinner one worked along the bight figure-eight fashion for several turns and finished with a half hitch around the standing part of the thick rope (Fig. 13B)—*line towing bend.*

When a rope is to be used as a heaving line, it is an advantage to have one end weighted slightly. Obviously, if the rope is to be thrown to another person the weight should not be too great or too hard. A large knot in the rope itself provides sufficient weight. The classic knot for this purpose is the *monkey's fist.* This is made of three interlocking hanks, usually of two or three turns each. Make up a hank of two or three turns, then wrap more turns loosely around the center (Fig. 13C). Add

BINDER TURN

LINE-TOWING BEND

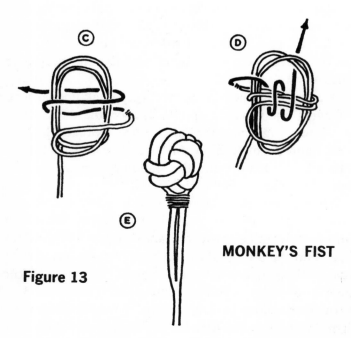

MONKEY'S FIST

Figure 13

more turns around these second turns and through the first turns (Fig. 13D). Work the whole thing tight by drawing through the rope with a spike. Either cut off the short end or splice it back into the standing part (Fig. 13E). To make the knot larger it is possible to include a small ball in the knot before tightening.

The monkey's fist is a fairly permanent weight. If something temporary and more quickly made is required, there is a variation on the hangman's knot—the *end-weight knot*—which can provide weight where it is re-

Figure 13
(cont.)

END-WEIGHT KNOT

quired. A length of rope is formed into a long S-shape, then the end is taken through the loop at the end and wrapped many times around the S (Fig. 13F). At the other end of the knot, the end of the rope is tucked through the opposite loop (Fig. 13G), which is drawn tight by pulling the first loop. This, in turn, is drawn tight by pulling the standing part.

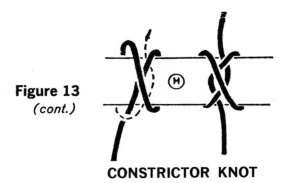

Figure 13
(cont.)

CONSTRICTOR KNOT

A very useful knot for drawing a bag tight, pulling several loose things together, or as a temporary whipping, is the *constrictor knot*. A turn is put on, as if starting a clove hitch, but the working end is then wrapped around the standing part under the cross part (Fig. 13H). When the two ends are pulled, the cross part bears down on the knot and prevents slip.

A knot which is sometimes confused with the rolling hitch is the *magnus hitch* (Fig. 13, I-L). Its use is the same as the clove hitch when extra security is needed, but the rolling hitch is used when the load comes along the spar. The magnus hitch has all the parts covered by one turn—in the rolling hitch the loaded part is covered by two turns.

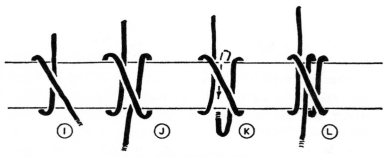

Figure 13
(cont.)   **MAGNUS HITCH**

An interesting method of interlocking loops is found in the *jury knot*. Three loops are formed (Fig. 14A). The two inner parts are drawn through as shown and the top of the center loop pulled upwards (Fig. 14B). This results in three loops and two ends equally spaced around the center (Fig. 14C).

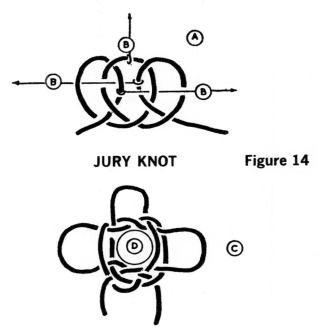

JURY KNOT   **Figure 14**

The original object of this knot is to provide loops to take stays at the top of a jury mast (a temporary one). The ends are tied to make a fourth loop. The stronger the pull on the loops, the tighter it grips the mast which stands through the center of the knot (Fig. 14D). Another use of the knot is as a bottle sling with four handles. With the neck of the bottle in place of the mast, the knot pulls tight and grips the bottle. In the days of our wooden-wall battleships, this knot was used for lifting round shot, which rested on the center, and the loops were drawn together by a sling above the shot.

A barrel or similar thing is simply arranged for lifting with an overhand knot. The barrel stands on the rope, and the two parts are made into an overhand knot above the barrel (Fig. 14E). This is opened out and the crossings adjusted down the sides of the barrel, then the ends are knotted together (Fig. 14F).

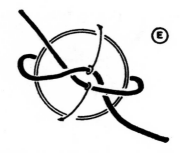

OVERHAND KNOT ON A BARREL

Figure 14 *(cont.)*

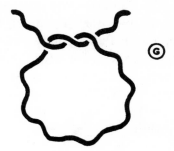

MAKING A QUOIT FROM A STRAND

Figure 14
(cont.)

A continuous rope, such as a grommet or quoit, is made from a single strand. Unlay a piece of rope at least ten times the intended diameter of the grommet. This will make three grommets. Be careful not to disturb the natural twist of the unlaid strand. Start laying this up around itself (Fig. 14G), fitting into the lay. Continue round until, after two circuits, you have a three-strand rope and the ends have met (Fig. 14H). Taper the strands to half thickness where they cross. Knot them together and tuck them into the adjoining strands.

Weights are moved by tackle which gives the operator an advantage, but there are two simple ways of shifting weights which do not need special apparatus. An article which is round and can be rolled may be *parbuckled*

(Fig. 14I). The center of the rope must be anchored to a holdfast, the two parts go under the object and the ends to the operator. Pulling on the ends gives him a two-fold advantage, except for slight frictional losses. A

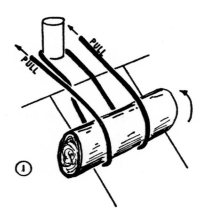

PARBUCKLING

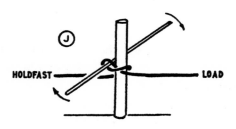

SPANISH WINDLASS

Figure 14 *(cont.)*

Spanish windlass may be used to shift a load horizontally. A rope from the load to a holdfast is looped with a short stick around a pole being held upright (Fig. 14J). If the stick is turned around the pole, considerable leverage can be applied.

8
Fancy Work

Cordage can be made up into many ornamental patterns, such as fancy knots, plaits and sennets, fringe work and woven patterns. Some of this work is very intricate and akin to knitting, crochet and tatting. A knowledge of the simpler fancy work is worth having, as you can make such things as buttons, dog leads, lanyards and scarf rings, as well as add decorative touches to more utilitarian rope work.

Much of the ornamental rope work was evolved by sailing ship seamen, looking for an activity to while away their spare time. Little of this work is seen afloat today, but one place where it survives is on the canal boat, where there are still Turk's heads and plaited ropes at stem and rudder head.

Fancy knotting may be done in any rope or cord, but for small practice work, colored blind cord is very effective, and the white cord sold by tool shops as builders' chalk line makes attractive plaits.

The best known fancy knot is the *Turk's head*. There are many variations, but the basic one is a continuous three plait, usually of two or three parts. If a stiff cord or thong is used, the knot may stand on its own and be used as a scarf ring or serviette ring. It may be done tightly around a pole or other solid object.

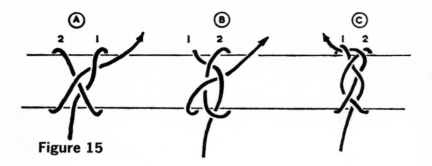

Figure 15

For a first attempt, work around a stick or over two fingers of the left hand. Start as if making a clove hitch, but instead of taking the working end under the crossing, go over it and under the first turn (Fig. 15A). Push the first turn under the second (Fig. 15B), then pass the working end over the second and under the first turn (Fig. 15C).

This is the complete set of actions. For a small ring the working end is taken in alongside the starting end (Fig. 15D) and followed around alongside it two or three times (Fig. 15E). If the cord is thin in relation to the thing it encircles, the set of actions may be repeated to increase the amount of plaiting, but it must be a complete set, bringing the working end to the left at the end again.

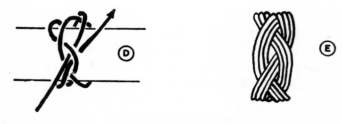

Figure 15
(cont.)

TURK'S HEAD

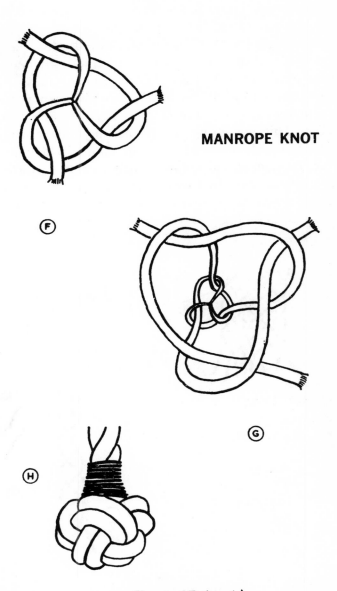

MANROPE KNOT

(F)

(G)

(H)

Figure 15 *(cont.)*

A *manrope knot* is a knob on the end of a rope made with the strands of the rope in a plaited form looking something like a Turk's head. The strands are separated and first tied in a wall knot—each strand is passed up under the next one (Fig. 15F) and pulled fairly tight. Going the same way round, the strands are next made into a crown knot (Fig. 15G), as if starting a back splice. This will bring the strands pointing down the rope alongside parts of the wall knot. To double the knot, let each strand follow its neighboring part around the wall and then the crown. The ends may be cut off, or pushed down through the center of the knot and whipped over the rope (Fig. 15H).

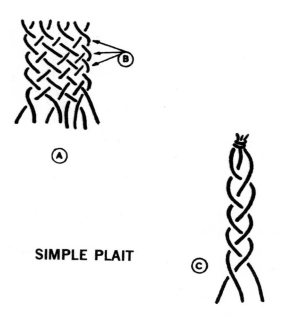

Ⓐ

Ⓑ

SIMPLE PLAIT

Ⓒ

Figure 16

The simplest plait, known as a *simple plait,* is a flat one made with any number of strands taken alternately over and under each other in a weaving pattern (Fig. 16A). As each strand reaches the side, it turns back (Fig. 16B). The commonest form of this plait is with three strands (Fig. 16C), but it is more effective with a greater number.

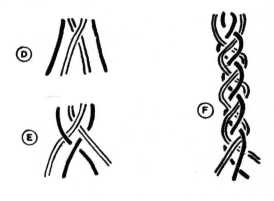

LARIAT PLAIT

Figure 16 *(cont.)*

A *lariat plait* is a flexible form of working four strands together. Some telephone leads are made up in this way. Knot the ends together and select opposite pairs, which will be worked in turn. Cross two between the other two (Fig. 16D), then cross the other two between them (Fig. 16E). Continue in this way, keeping the crossings close against those already done for the best appearance (Fig. 16F), although if flexibility is important, the plait may be more drawn out.

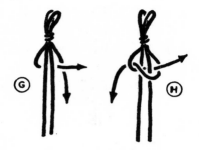

BOS'N'S PLAIT . . .

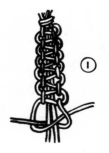

FLAT . . .

Figure 16 *(cont.)*

The *bos'n's plait,* or *Portuguese sennit,* is very decorative. It is worked with two strands around a core. The core may be a piece of wood, a leather thong or another rope. A neat plait is made if the core is made of a pair

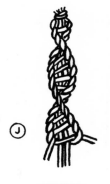

Figure 16
(cont.)

Ⓙ

SPIRAL

of cords the same as is used for plaiting. A considerable length is used up in this plait, so the core strands should only be about a sixth of the length of the working parts.

For a practice plait, knot four ends together, then hook the two core strands to your belt so that you can keep them tensioned. The two outside pieces are made into a series of overhand knots. Pass the left piece behind the core and let the right piece hang behind that (Fig. 16G). Lift the right piece across the core and down through the loop of the first (Fig. 16H). Pull outwards to tighten.

To make a *flat bos'n's plait* repeat the actions the opposite way—pass the right piece behind the core and take the left piece across and through its loop. In effect you are tying reef knots, and the result will be a naturally flat stiff plait (Fig. 16I). If you repeat the actions all one way, you will be tying granny knots, and the plait will automatically develop into a *spiral* (Fig. 16J).

A plait which mystifies is a flat three plait made in strands without ends. This is seen in the *Scouts' woggle,* or *scarf ring,* made by slitting a piece of leather. Work from the top as though working in three separate strands.

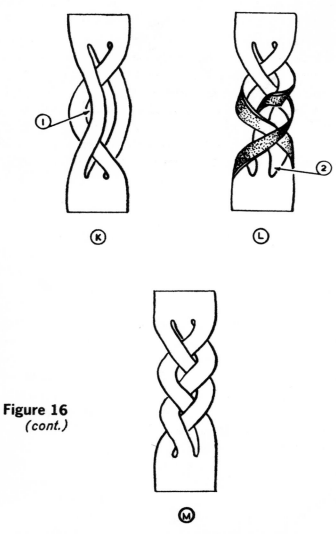

Figure 16
(cont.)

SCOUT'S WOGGLE OR SCARF RING

The problem comes in dealing with the tangle which develops at the bottom. Cross right over center, then left over right (Fig. 16K). Hold this in position and push the bottom completely through gap 1 (Fig. 16L), leaving the strands twisted. If you now push the bottom through gap 2, everything should come right (Fig. 16M). This is a complete set of actions and may be sufficient for a short piece, but the process can be repeated as often as necessary to fill a longer length. In a complete set of actions, each side strip goes to the other side and back again, and the center strip goes to both sides.